M000120496

METHODS OF HEALING THROUGH THE APPLICATION OF CONSCIOUSNESS

Svetlana Smirnova

and

Sergey Jelezky

SVET-Center, Hamburg

Jelezky Publishing
www.jelezky-publishing.com

First English Edition, January 2012

© 2012 English Language Edition
SVET Center, Hamburg
Svetlana Smirnova
www.svet-centre.eu

First English Edition, January 2012
© 2012 English Language Edition

Sergey Eletskiy, Hamburg (editor)

English Translation: Margarete and William Mieger

Cover Design: Sergey Jelezky
www.jelezky.com

© 2012 Copyright Svetlana Smirnova, Sergey Eletskiy

All rights reserved. The use of text and illustrations, also as excerpts, without the permission of the publisher is a violation of copyright law and punishable as such. This includes photocopies, translations, microfilm copies and data processing for electronic systems.

ISBN: 978-3-943110-34-0

Our special thanks to
Grigori Grabovoi
for making this book possible.

We also wish to thank our further teachers
Nadeshda and Vadim Korolov, Igor Arepjev and
Arcady Petrov for their comprehensive knowledge,
which has also found expression in this book.

Svetlana and Sergey

Spring, 2010

According to the responses we have received, the contents of this book have helped many people. We are confident that this will continue to be the case.

Nonetheless, we would like to point out that the techniques of Grigori Grabovoi are mental methods for the guidance of events in one's life. These methods are dependent upon one's personal spiritual development. Because we are dealing with topics relating to one's health, we give this express notice that such influence is not a "therapy" in the conventional sense of the word and is therefore not intended to limit or replace professional medical care.

When in doubt, follow the directions of your doctor or a therapist or pharmacist whom you trust! (When following conventional methods, you must expect to geconventional results.)

Jelelezky Publishing/SVET center, Hamburg

Disclaimer:

**The information within this book is intended as reference
material only, and not as medical or professional advice.**

Information contained herein is intended to give you the tools to make informed decisions about your lifestyle. It should not be used as a substitute for any treatment that has been prescribed or recommended by your qualified doctor. Do not stop taking any medication unless advised by your qualified doctor to do otherwise. The author and publisher are not healthcare professionals, and expressly disclaim any responsibility for any adverse effects occurring as a result of the use of suggestions or information in this book. This book is offered for your own education and enjoyment only. As always, never begin a health program without first consulting a **qualified healthcare professional.** Your use of this book indicates your agreement to these terms.

Table of Contents

© Svetlana Smirnova, 2012

Preface

Dear Reader,

We all live in an extraordinary time – a time of change from old values to the emergence of new knowledge. We observe the rapidly progressing research on man and his environment. Modern scientists have made an enormous number of new discoveries and have presented many revolutionary – and alternative – new theories.

It appears that modern science can protect humanity from virtually everything – new viruses and bacteria, stress and psychic "nervous breakdowns," ecological and technological catastrophes. However, the further modern science progresses in its knowledge, the more obvious it becomes that the territory of the unknown is without boundaries! Who can help us find the answers to a host of questions that are intimately connected with our daily life, with the search for the meaning of life, or with the hope for healing?

The teaching that we are writing about here may be known to one in part from various publications, another may be hearing about it for the first time. This knowledge emerged in 1992 when in Russia a number of institutes began research on the general deliverance and further harmonious development of the world (of perceptible reality). Since this time, it has enjoyed continuous further development and can boast of ongoing new results. People of varying religious conviction and of diverse languages are now speaking in the entire world of these results.

This teaching is based upon the assumption that the Creative Power (God), regardless of belief system and cultural orientation, exists

© Svetlana Smirnova, 2012

everywhere the same. It is not a new religion, but the knowledge behind creation itself that has been rediscovered and made known by Grigori Grabovoi. He says that both the world (outer reality) and ensouled mankind (inner reality) are informational structures: "When we consider the world, man within the world and how man develops in the world, we see that all change emanates from man. This means that the world, outer reality, develops by cause of man through his conscious or unconscious, inner reality."

Grigori Grabovoi has written three works on his insights in which the methods are described for the restoration and regeneration of organs as well as the healing of apparently incurable diseases, including such as AIDS and cancer. For many years now his methods are being practically applied in a number of countries. Many extraordinary healing successes have been documented and notarized. Grigori Grabovoi has proven to today's medical practice that there are no incurable diseases and that every disease, including cancer and AIDS, can be healed – even in the so-called "final stages."

Many of his students, including the authors – Svetlana Smirnova and Sergey Jelezky – have in the meantime, through the use of these methods for the restoration of health and harmonization of events in and around the patient, been able to achieve the same or similar results. In this context we would like to point out that in order to be successful, everyone must ultimately find those methods that work for oneself (or for others) from among the numerous methods presented here.

In this booklet we are presenting only those methods, which we have successfully employed with ourselves or with our patients. These

8

© Svetlana Smirnova, 2012

methods originate with Grigori Grabovoi and have been developed further by our colleagues, Nadeshda and Vadim Korolev (methods for working with any disease, spiritual healing of childhood diseases, restoration of the spine, the extruder, the structure of the soul). The methods for the restoration of teeth are from Arcady Petrov.

All of us at the SVET-Zentrum (Center) wish you the best of health and great success with all of your efforts! Please recall that all of the threads of your life lie in your and only in your hands. The tree of life, which exists in your consciousness, has both inner and outer connections with reality. Within the body, these are the connections of the brain with every organ and the connections with every cell and, more importantly, with the environment that sustain the balance critical for life.

Promote the good – for yourself and your surroundings. Think positively and everything will be good and harmonious with you. Your problems will resolve themselves, difficulties will dissolve into nothing and your rejuvenated and healed organism will become a support for your spirit for many, many years to come.

With heartfelt regards,
Svetlana Smirnova and Sergey Jelezky

SVET- Center, Hamburg

© Svetlana Smirnova, 2012

1.

Human!
You are the world, you are eternity.
You possess immeasurable powers.
Your possibilities are limitless.
You are the embodiment of the creator.

In you, his will resides,
through his destiny you change the world.
In you, his love resides.
Love all life as he does, he who has created you.
Do not embitter your heart. Think good, do good.
Good will return to you with longevity.
Love will give immortality,
faith and hope, prudence.

With faith and love
your invisible powers will come alive.
And you will achieve all that you dream of.
Immortality, it is the face of life.
Just as life is the trace of eternity.
Create to live in eternity.
Live to create eternity.

Grigori Grabovoi

© Svetlana Smirnova, 2012

2. How is it Possible to Completely Restore Man and the Perceptible World?

In his book "Applied Structures of the Creative Field of Information," Grigori Grabovoi describes how man is created. He describes how man, through his spiritual structures, stands in direct connection and interaction with the entire world (external reality). Through an understanding of the spiritual relationships and structures, one comes to the knowledge that every person is directly and inextricably connected with the entire world and through his thinking, feeling and actions becomes the cause of an effect, a change, in the world. Similarly, a change in the outer reality leads to a change in the inner reality, within man. Grabovoi names the following assumptions:

First: The entire world has an informational structure.
Second: Man is a structure of light that harbors information within itself.
Third: In man there are three divine structures:
            the soul,
            the spirit,
            consciousness.

Man, as well as the world, is built entirely out of this triad. And so man can be restored on the so-called information level on which his original matrix exists according to the perfect plan of Creation. But why is it important that a person learns to restore himself?

When man restores himself, that is enters into harmony and the divine norm, he restores his surroundings at the same time and

© Svetlana Smirnova, 2012   11

brings them into harmony with himself. When the surroundings are restored, that is, brought into harmony and the divine norm, the person who is restoring them is also brought into harmony and the norm. Man has thus the unique opportunity to create change through the application of his consciousness and to transform any negative information (information lying outside of the norm) in either the inner or outer reality into positive information (information according to the norm).

According to present knowledge, the world is constructed as follows:

The soul creates light and information. The spirit transfers this information from the soul to consciousness. Consciousness takes on the information and manifests it in the form of objects (matter), which we perceive around us as form. When man changes information, he changes the world – and himself.

The world is directly dependent upon the consciousness of man. In order to change the world, man's desire for self-knowledge is already sufficient. Knowing himself, man finds his way to Creation, to God. Only in the course of self-discovery can man communicate directly with God and the Creation.

One person seeks God in Tibet, another in India, another in the cosmos and so on. But God is to be found within every person and in his soul. The soul is a part of Creation, a part of God, and it is through the spirit and consciousness that everything, which has a soul in the world of experience, is manifested.

When a person develops spiritually, he finds his way to God and recognizes the Creation in all that is. In this manner man attains to limitless creative powers and possibilities. Grigori Grabovoi says that

12   © Svetlana Smirnova, 2012

every person is able to use this knowledge and come to the desired result through its application.

Regeneration of a "lost" organ is possible, because the information about the healthy organ remains stored for all time in an information field. The physical human body is a manifested structure that develops out of the information structure of a primal matrix predetermined by Creation. We also say that we are the "children" of God or that we are made in His "image."

In the soul of man there is an archiving point, in which all information about his individuality is retained. By working with the knowledge of the archiving point, essentially every person can be renewed. Initiating the process of renewal requires no more than an impulse of light from one's soul. A person's mere desire to help himself or someone else is already sufficient to impart an impulse from the soul. But there is an important condition attached to visible success: belief in the Creation.

In order to be able to restore a lost organ, belief in a God, who is present in each and every thing as its Creation, is necessary. If a person does not hold this belief, all effort is in vain. The world is God and God is the world! Everything we perceive around us – including ourselves – is an expression of God and His Creation. With the dawn of this recognition, a person acquires the ability through his soul to exert an influence on his health and the events in his life!

© Svetlana Smirnova, 2012

13

3. The Soul – the Spirit – Consciousness

The Soul:

The soul is the plane of interaction with the Creator. The inner and outer, the finite and the heavenly worlds, can be found on this plane. Every star in the sky is a soul. The soul is as firm and unshakeable as the creational matrix of the world itself, which organizes everything. The action of the soul is the movement of the spirit and the measurement of the spirit's movement in our dimension is time and space. This action is reflected in mind. Mind is like the planets: they do not produce light; they reflect it.

Every person has a soul, that is, a portion of eternity, within himself: a world of deliverance, peace and love. The soul should always be considered as primal, that is proceeding from the Creator. What does it mean to be a "human being?" It means to strive to be and to be of like nature with one's Creator. It means: to be conform with the ideal. To create as the Creator creates. To be wise as He is wise. To love as He loves.

"Through consciousness the soul creates the form of existence." (G.G.)

Everything that has form and primal existence has been created through the structure of the soul: stars, planets, life. Everything emanates from us and has been created with the help of the reflection of consciousness. It appears as a mirror of the soul. The soul is the principle, mind the structure, and the Creator provides the basis for everything. He created these principles, this structure and everything that came from it.

© Svetlana Smirnova, 2012

From the soul, the principle that He created, comes the development of everything in us, on the earth and in the universe. When we understand these principles, we will also understand the structure and then we can make use of it.

Primary information is transferred from the soul and reflected into the external, "secondary" world through the replicating action of consciousness. The organization of this evolution is then detailed through the interaction of the individual subject with its objects. It is there, where the inner world touches the outer world, that awareness gives rise to understanding. In the moment that consciousness performs an act of awareness, information from the plane of the spirit is projected and transformed into external structure. In this manner objective reality is created on the screen of subjective reality. The soul, which disburses primal knowledge through the spirit, expands the mind. Mind – through the action of the spirit – reacts, grasps, realizes and expands itself in the act of creating and building the structure of the world.

The Spirit:

Spirit is the form in which the soul takes action. It is an energy reservoir for the construction of reality. When the spirit conceives the form of an object, the physical body of God appears as a manifestation, in the outer macro-reality as well as the inner micro-reality. The activity of the spirit on the physical plane is what produces both growth and delimitation. The cells divide with the help of the spirit; without the spirit, they can only disintegrate. Spirit is life. There is life within every object and every living being. Spirit is everywhere and in everything. It is not a little cloud as some people imagine. It is energy that is organized and that has a structure.

© Svetlana Smirnova, 2012   15

We turn the TV on and the screen lights up. If we make this analogy with the human being, the screen is awareness. But only as an analogy, for man's awareness is immeasurably higher and more complex: it is the principle of the projection of the idea of the universe into infinity. Spirit is what allows the screen to function, to carry out its task!

Spirit is the connection between the non-visible within the soul and the visible world of the mind. Spirit is the force and spirit is like a stream of neutrinos (neutral subatomic particles) for which there are no obstacles and which penetrate everything in their surroundings.

Neither the density of the earth nor artificial barriers can halt the spirit. It is omnipresent, permeating everything while damaging nothing. It allows for the appearance, the existence of everything.

"The Spirit goes wherever it pleases."
(from the Bible)

Consciousness:

Consciousness is the general ability to process information and react to it. But consciousness operates in various states: sleeping, waking and expanded. Expanded consciousness has at its disposal a measurable world of numerous dimensions. And then there is also true, higher consciousness. All of the different levels have their special characteristics.

Normal consciousness perceives as reality that which has been historically mirrored and stored and exists in our mind in this form. Our view of the world around us is a result of the sum of the views of those who live in it. You might say that the general worldview is nothing more than a parable about us all, a fable convenue.

Expanded consciousness arises in the perception of the interactions

16   © Svetlana Smirnova, 2012

between the visible and non-visible worlds. This state of consciousness is capable of perceiving the processes of both of these realms. It is also able to guide these processes on both the micro and macro levels in all of their respective nuances.

True, higher consciousness mirrors the entire structure of the world and is capable of manifesting any chosen element of reality.

What is expanded consciousness good for? For knowing and for seeing. Here we are referring to "spiritual sight." People in the state of normal consciousness perceive the world differently, as though they were lost in the dark. They fall, stand up, and fall again, this time hitting themselves in the head and breaking their nose. Is this freedom or only an illusion of freedom?

"You must know where you are going.
You must know the way – this is freedom."

Becoming conscious is primarily a matter of grasping the nature of one's own self, one's own personality. When a person reaches the level of genuine truth, he attains to the possibility of influencing his psychophysical and mental abilities as well as changing the course of physical events. This is possible because all processes in the world are connected to the global factor "man."

This means that man himself is the source. Receiving an impulse, processing the impulse and sending the impulse forth to create something out of matter or to create some change; these are all functions of consciousness and its general capabilities: receiving information – processing – reacting to the information! On the level of thought impulses, soul, spirit and consciousness can solve any problem – sometimes even instantaneously!

Dr. Grigori Grabovoi has described various technologies of working with consciousness in his works. This booklet is based upon the results achieved by this exceptional scholar, clairvoyant and healer. Consciousness is a generalized reaction of the subject to his informational surroundings. It only appears where information is, be this externally and/or internally. Therefore consciousness possesses, according also to a general understanding, a structure that unites spiritual (non-material) and physical (material) reality.

The ability, via soul and spirit, to work with consciousness can lead to radical changes of the subject as well as the object. For now it is not the environment that is determining the structure of man, but man who is determining the structure of his world. This is exactly what happens when people who are suffering from some malaise come to us: we correct the subjective situation of a specific person in the world because everything in the world is build upon the basis of consciousness. And consciousness can, with the help of the soul and the spirit, influence any and every element of reality.

18

© Svetlana Smirnova, 2012

4. "Spiritual" Healing of Childhood Diseases

(Nadeshda Korolova, Vadim Korolov)

In the future our medical practice will change: from a preference for a physical treatment of the body to methods of spiritual and mental healing. Treatment will be carried out by those who are able to restore the harmony between the soul and consciousness – or hinder a disharmony from occurring right from the start. In the long run these methods will also remove the roots of disease.

In this age of technocratic technologies man has come to a point at which he is capable of destroying himself and all of humanity. There are examples enough for this. People are coming down more often with oncological diseases (cancers) than with the flu and hundreds of thousands of children die every day because there are no medicines that can heal them from the most serious of diseases. Man begins more and more often to turn to God. Why?

People pray for help, health, luck, success and many other things. People pray to their Creator for that which everyone and everyone alike has already received from him originally. Only a few pray to God to give them the knowledge of who they are, who we are. We – mankind! Only a few ask: what are the possibilities available to us and how can and should we apply these god-given potentials – to help ourselves and also others? At the SVET-Zentrum, we offer concrete technologies that simply work, as long as a person has a belief in God, in himself and in his divine origins. Let us consider the situation through an example, the childhood disease of scarlet fever.

The children who contract this disease are usually between the ages of three to eight years. This is the age in which the child perceives the

© Svetlana Smirnova, 2012

world directly through the soul. Its soul makes a prognosis of events 14 days in advance. When you look at the time from the moment the illness begins up to when it is overcome, you come to the understanding that the child sees the negative future events in its surroundings that could happen, for example with its relatives, and begins to process these through the illness. The child processes in this manner the future events and the relationships between its parents and between its relatives. In this way it attempts to direct its awareness (unconsciously) to these future events in order to create an understanding for the situation.

But in order to understand the child, you must first go the path of expanded spiritual development, the "path of knowledge." The parents have no idea, of course, why their child has become ill. Conventional medicine says the disease has come by way of infection. It is assumed that the child has had contact with someone who has the disease and that the child was "infected." But this is not quite right!

The smaller the child is, the greater the probability of coming down with this disease. Children (people) come into this world with the task of making it better, of transforming and purifying negativity, of creating in a heartfelt and imaginative manner. It is thought that with children their immunity is only weakly developed. We think that this is not so! The consciousness of children is still relatively unstructured. The child acts directly from the soul, but the tool of creating is consciousness. The child's consciousness cannot yet adequately "cope" with the world it is encountering and so it can become ill.

Let us take a look at a second variation in which the child is going to kindergarten or to school. Children that go to such institutions begin to help each other out, that is, they take on the problems of a child who has become ill and try in this way to help him. They also begin to get sick. If

20   © Svetlana Smirnova, 2012

the disease is not yet physically visible, this does not mean that children are not aware of it. One child sees the problem in the external world and on the soul level says to the sick child: "I will help you" – and starts to help. And a second and a third child join in.

Now one might ask why don't all of the children get sick? The answer is simply that children do not only gather knowledge on the physical plane, but primarily on the spiritual plane. The one child is satisfied with merely observing and has thereby already understood everything. Another child has to first go through the course of events. In this manner children learn how one can act in this or the other situation, how one creates relationships and how these appear and are experienced in the external and internal worlds.

In either case the person attains to knowledge and in the physical world the child begins with incredible speed to regain that knowledge, which was extinguished at birth. Once the child has gone through certain diseases, immunity develops. Immunity is nothing more than the knowledge that has come from the soul by way of the spirit and consciousness. Once a child has gone through these experiences on the spiritual plane, it knows exactly how it must construct the relationships and events in its own future life.

How can this situation be generally avoided and the normal condition of health preserved? You need only develop your ability for spiritual sight in order for parents and children to transform any situation, including its form of appearance on the physical plane. In reference to childhood diseases, we can say: one must give a direction to the future events by deepening the relationship between the parents and of the children to their parents. Here it is events that have a direct relationship

© Svetlana Smirnova, 2012

to or direct influence on the family that play an important role. These relationships must, of course, be corrected gently and lovingly, even without any particular spiritual understanding of the guidance of events through the application of consciousness.

© Svetlana Smirnova, 2012

5. Dependable Guidance of Events through Numbers
(Grigori Grabovoi)

Behind every number is a corresponding vibrational structure. The same is true for number sequences. The number sequences, which are given in Grabovoi's works "Concentration Exercises" and "Restoration of the Human Organism through Concentration on Numbers" are connected with a guiding force that emanates from the spiritual plane. It is for this reason that working with these numbers contributes to one's spiritual development. The number sequences support a structuring of consciousness for the guidance of events.

When you concentrate on the numbers, you should consciously become aware of yourself, feel your own organism, look at it mentally – see it absolutely healthy! This is important for the rapid restoration of a normal condition of health (according to the norm of the Creator).

One can fundamentally say that there is a spiritual-energetic vibrational component to every number. This is the cause of their ability to effect a change. There is also a spiritual-energetic vibrational component to every word and every sound. There are regions of man's consciousness that are connected to every number. The concentration on a particular number creates a vibration in its corresponding area. The language in which a number is named and spoken out is not of consequence here.

Pay attention to the following important moment!

You must understand that the effectiveness of your focus is primarily dependent upon your mindset during your concentration session. Open yourself to this creative process. Listen to your inner voice, which will

© Svetlana Smirnova, 2012   23

prompt you in the practical aspects of your concentration. You can, for example, simply write the number sequence on a piece of paper and direct your focus to it.

But you can also do it differently. For example, with a focus upon a nine-digit number sequence, you can imagine that you are in the middle of a sphere and the numbers are written on its inner surface. The information about your concentration goal (for example the healing of a person) is located in another smaller sphere, which is within the larger sphere with the numbers. Focus on finding which number shines the brightest for you. The moment the first thought impulse points you to a number on the inner surface of the sphere that shines brighter than the others, fix your attention on this number! Then mentally connect the smaller sphere with your concentration goal (health) and the element of receptivity in the form of this number and the healing process has been put into motion.

When focusing upon a sequence of 7 digits, you can for example imagine that the numbers are located on one of the sides of a cube. You can move the numbers around on the cube according to your feeling of where they belong until the maximal effect for you is achieved.

© Svetlana Smirnova, 2012

6. The Healing of any Disease with the Help of Number Sequences
(Grigori Grabovoi)

This method of healing through the use of number sequences is simple and very effective. The process is described by Grigori Grabovoi in his book "Restoration of the Human Organism through Concentration on Numbers." Approximately 1,000 medical diagnoses are listed in this book and each disease has a correlating number sequence. The sequences consist of 7, 8 or 9 numbers. While you concentrate upon a specific number sequence, you are healing yourself of its corresponding disease. Now the question can arise: Why is such a simple act as concentrating upon a number sequence so effective?

The significant factor here is that every disease represents a departure from the norm. This deviance from the norm can be in the body's cells, its organs or in the functioning of the entire organism. Healing the disease requires a restoration of the body to the norm. The number sequences promote the restoration process. While you are working with the number sequences and focusing upon them, you are tuning in to a state that embodies the norm. This results in a healing of the disease. To better understand the process of this form of healing, let us take a look at the vibrational aspect of numbers. Our life runs a rhythmical course. Planets circle the sun in periodic orbits. For Earth, this leads to a constant alternation of spring, summer, fall and winter. The Earth turns on its axis and we experience day and night. The same sort of thing occurs also on a micro level. Electrons circle in defined paths and rhythmical movements around the nucleus of the atom. Each of us can hear and feel the rhythmical beat of our heart. In our body every cell

© Svetlana Smirnova, 2012

has its own rhythm and the entirety of all cells also has its own rhythm. Beyond this, there is a rhythm on the level of the relationship of the organs to each other.

You could compare our organism with an orchestra, in which every musician plays according to a given score and yet together they create harmonious music. The orchestra as a whole sounds differently than each musician with his instrument alone. If just one musician plays something wrong, the harmony of the whole is disturbed. This is how it is in the human organism. The rhythm of each specific organ, even each cell in the organism, disturbs or creates harmony in the entire body – ideally none will play a wrong tone, but all will play together harmoniously. The tones within our body can be harmonious all of the time. If an organ or a function in the body departs from the norm, there is a disharmony in the whole body – a discomfort or a disease. We are the conductor of this orchestra and the one who through soul, spirit and consciousness can restore harmony to the body.

This aspect of numbers can also be observed where it is not obvious at first look. Consider the rainbow. We see intense, beautiful colors. But what do these colors represent from a scientific perspective? Our perception of color is based upon an effect of electromagnetic radiation of various frequencies. The frequency of the color violet is, for example, a doubling of the frequency of the color red. Every color has its own frequency or vibration. All of the images that we see on TV are a mixture of three colors: red, green and blue. The optimal image quality is created when each of the three colors occurs in a different proportion and brightness. Each new color choice from the spectrum produces its own special effect.

The same can be said of number sequences. You can look at each number as a frequency and each sequence as a certain pattern of

26

© Svetlana Smirnova, 2012

frequencies or vibrations. If the seating distribution on an airline flight is not harmonious, the balance of the entire load can be disrupted and lead to undesirable vibration. A balanced seating distribution harmonizes and stabilizes the flight.

About the book with the catalog of number sequences *(Restoration of the Human Organism through Concentration on Numbers):*

This book consists of 27 chapters. Each chapter deals with a diagnostic category of specific conditions. The first 25 chapters contain a complete overview of all diseases. After each chapter title there is a number sequence that pertains to all of the conditions in that chapter. You can always use this number sequence and particularly then, when the precise diagnosis is missing. It can happen that you only know that your condition belongs to a particular category! If the diagnosis is clearly stated, then start with the corresponding number sequence. In the book this number sequence immediately follows the designation of the diagnosis.

Number sequences for unknown diseases are listed in Chapter 26 with a number sequence for each of seven areas of the body. In this case take the number sequence for the area of the body in which your condition is located.

About the application and use of these number sequences:

Let's assume that someone has a headache. First, you can take the number sequence for the head (Chapter 26). If you have pain in more than one part of the body, focus upon the number sequence for each location, one after the other.

Now let's take a look at the sequences themselves, which consist of 7, 8 or 9 digits. If the number sequence consists of 9 digits, then one or

© Svetlana Smirnova, 2012

two specific diseases can be healed with this sequence. If the number sequence consists of 8 digits, then five or more diseases can be healed with this sequence. If the number sequence consists of 7 digits, then this sequence can heal ten or more diseases. The seven-digit sequences cover more possibilities than the others. This is also a reason why they are the basis of the system Grabovoi employs in *Restoration of the Human Organism through Concentration on Numbers*.

You can work through the number sequence from left to right from number to number, or from right to left, or you can start at both ends of the sequence and work towards the middle. In working with the number sequences, you can structure your focus in various ways. You can either focus on each number for the same length of time or for differing lengths of time, whatever suits you best. When you change the length of time of the focus on a particular number, you change the intensity of this number's participation in the healing. For this reason every period of concentration produces a different effect. It is best to trust your intuition during the focus. The restorative effect of the focus will be produced regardless of the variations used in a particular session.

© Svetlana Smirnova, 2012

Area of the Condition	Number Sequence
Unknown conditions in general(*)	1884321
Head	1819999
Neck	18548321
Right arm, right hand	1854322
Left arm, left hand	4851384
Torso	5185213
Right leg, right foot	4812531
Left leg, left foot	485148291

(* With unknown conditions, use also the sequence for the body location)

Some examples of known conditions from the catalog in the book "Restoration of the Human Organism through Concentration on Numbers":

Disease	Number Sequence
Allergies	45143212
Arthritis	8111110
Asthma bronchiale	8943548
Wounds	5148912

Other interesting number sequences

(not contained in the book):

Topic (Problem)	Sequence	Concentration Goal
Harmonizing of the present	71042	determined personally
Harmonizing of the future	148721091	determined personally
Harmonizing of the past	7819019425	determined personally
Plants	811120218	determined personally
Animals	555142198110	determined personally

© Svetlana Smirnova, 2012

Improving financial situations *	71427321893	determined personally
Solving general problems *	212309909	determined personally
Harmonizing family relationships	285555901	determined personally
Harmonizing a situation at work	141111963	determined personally
Goal orientation of children when learning	212585212	determined personally
Transformation of something negative to something positive	1888948	determined personally

(* To improve your focus, surround yourself with the corresponding number sequence: put a copy into your wallet, your passport or some other convenient location. Place the number sequence in your workspace or home.)

Further interesting number sequences / Concentration on a body location:

Indication	Sequence	Concentrate on ...
Critical conditions	1258912	the eyes and then on the most distant objects of the external world
Acute cardiovascular insuffici-ency (acute heart failure)	1895678	the right leg, the big toe of the left foot and the left ear
Traumatic shock, shock and shock-like conditions	1895132	the right eye, the left ear and the right little toe
Tumors (benign)	18584321	the skin of the hands and the feet in general
Tumors (malignant)	8214351	the surface of the skin of the soles of both feet and the left underarm

© Svetlana Smirnova, 2012

Sepsis	58143212	the underside of the right arm and on the most distant objects of the external world
Respiratory diseases	5823214	the right leg and the little finger of the left hand
Diseases of the digestive system	5321482	the right ear
Diseases of the kidneys and urinary tract	8941254	the right knee joint
Endocrine and metabolic disorders	1823451	the transition zones between our physical body and the external world
Occupational diseases	4185481	one's own saliva
Acute toxication	4185412	the right ear and on the left knee joint
Infectious diseases	5421427	the right ear and the eyelashes of the right eye
Neurological diseases	148543293	the right pointer finger
Dermatological (skin) and venereal diseases	18584321	(one after the other) on both hands, both legs, then the right eye
Surgical diseases	18574321	the spine, the right leg and the sole of the left foot
Diseases of the eyes	1891014	the eyes and the coccyx area of the spine
Diseases of the teeth and oral cavity	1488514	the teeth and the little finger of the left hand

© Svetlana Smirnova, 2012

7. The Technology of Rejuvenation
(Grigori Grabovoi)

Find a photo of yourself in which you are young and happy. Hold it in front of yourself at eye level. Now picture the following number sequences in the space between your face and the photo, on the level of your forehead, and focus on them:

2145432   and   **2213445**

Now also illuminate the number sequences with a silvery-white light. If you like, you can write the two number sequences on the photo above your head. While concentrating upon the photo, remember the happiest moment of your youth, your present moment and your future (your dreams). Do this several times a day until it has become anchored in your consciousness. After this, repeat as often as you desire.

© Svetlana Smirnova, 2012

8. The Area of Information Creation
(Grigori Grabovoi)

There is a place in the energetic structure of man located between the 1-meter (approx. 3 feet) sphere and the 5-meter sphere (approx. 16 feet) of our consciousness where information creates reality. Let us first construct the geometry of this realm in which we are going to work:

1. Mentally construct a sphere with the radius of 5 meters with yourself as the center (Fig. 1),

2. Now make a copy of the first sphere and reduce its radius down to 1 meter (Fig. 2).

With the help of these two spheres, it is possible to influence both informational and physical aspects of reality. The center of the two spheres is located near the geometrical center of our physical body. One center is located in the area of the heart and the other is slightly to one side in the center of the chest.

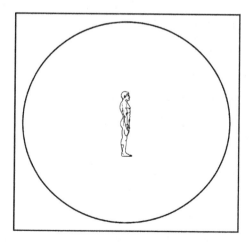

Fig. 1

© Svetlana Smirnova, 2012

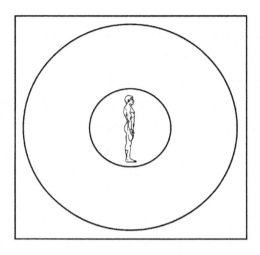

Fig. 2

When working on guiding the outcome of situations, however, we only consider that portion of the spheres that extends outward in front of our physical body from the area of the chest. Of course, the spheres also exist behind the body, but we do not use this portion of the spheres because this area is reserved for control. Mental involvement of this part of the spheres should only be used as an exception in special cases.

It is important to recall that the physical body is also an element of our perceptions. In the process we do not use any knowledge taken from the fields of morphology or anatomy; we only use information taken from the realm that we can see with our eyes. We take the space within the 1-meter sphere as the area for our perception. The specific area used within this sphere is selected as follows:

We picture waves of information (light waves) that originate between

34   © Svetlana Smirnova, 2012

our eyebrows and are sent out from this location. These waves are reflected from the inner surface of the 5-meter sphere back to the outer surface of the 1-meter sphere. In this manner we discover a wave path that corresponds geometrically to our realm of perception (Fig. 3).

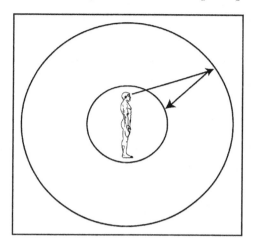

Fig. 3

But how do we work with the The Area of Information Creation ? Any information that exists around a person could be taken as an illustration, but here we will show how information can be transformed through the example of a flu epidemic:

Because the individual afflicted by this disease represents the micro level, we first go out to the macro level (flu is a collective phenomenon), that is, we go beyond the 5-meter sphere of the informational realm of our consciousness. We go out to the macro level so that the information of an abnormal situation (in reference to the norm of Creation) does not overwhelm a person.

Man is larger and stronger on the macro level. One is now looking from the macro level at the micro level, from a place beyond the

© Svetlana Smirnova, 2012

"danger zone" for the flu epidemic.

To reach the macro level, simply say (mentally):

"I go now to the macro level."

Now we start to locate and prepare the area that is responsible for the anomaly. It lies between a segment of the outside of the 1-meter sphere and a segment of the inside of the 5-meter sphere. We say:

"I see the segment, which is responsible for the information of the anomaly on the outside of the 1-meter sphere."

We mentally mark this segment and say further:

"I see the segment, which is responsible for the information of the anomaly on the inside of the 5-meter sphere."

We also mark this segment mentally, connect the ends of both segments, and inscribe the internal informational space with the sign of the Christ, the letter X, which symbolizes a diagonal symmetry in harmony with the Creation (Fig. 4) or we write the word "NORM" in this area (Fig. 5). At the same time we illuminate the area with a silvery-white light.

In this manner we have designated that portion of the the Area of Information Creation responsible for the anomaly, consolidated the information and transformed all of the abnormal information into information that conforms to the norm of the Creator.

Now we enter in the time and the date and send the positive information

© Svetlana Smirnova, 2012

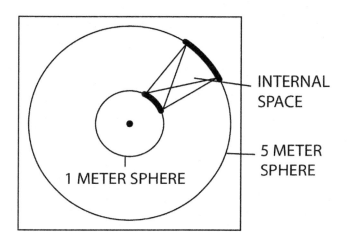

Fig. 4

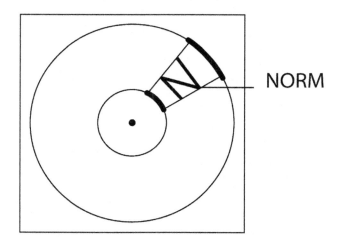

Fig. 5

© Svetlana Smirnova, 2012

into infinity. In this manner we have designated the point in time from which this information begins to spread throughout the world.

© Svetlana Smirnova, 2012

9. Basic Methods for Working with any Disease

(Nadeshda Korolova, Vadim Korolov)

When information enters the organism, it makes perforations on a person's 1-meter sphere. They look like dots or even holes in the surface of the sphere. It is possible to restore the surface to its original condition. We create a "light patch" for the punctures with the light of the Holy Spirit. We then say:

"Regeneration to the norm for all perforations."

Every disease has its informational structure. Once we have removed the point(s) of penetration, we remove their informational structure by saying:

"I see the informational structure of the disease and surround it with a sphere of silvery-white light (or with "hot plasma"). I compress it into a single point, take it outside of the border of the 5-meter sphere and place it into a silvery-white cube for the transformation of all negative information into positive information."

It is desirable to take all informational structures that are connected with the disease beyond the 5-meter sphere into the silvery-white cube. This cube is a secure space into which all negative information can be placed for the purpose of transformation. This is the method for extracting (transforming) the informational structure of a disease.

Finally we remove the leading cell. We surround it with a sphere of

© Svetlana Smirnova, 2012

39

hot plasma while compressing the leading cell into a single point and take it outside of the border of the 5-meter sphere. Because we have removed a cell, we must immediately reestablish a new cell from living matter.

We insert the cell with living matter in the place where the leading cell was. From this new cell we send information to all of the other cells. This means that when we remove negative information, it is absolutely necessary to install positive information in its place. We say:

"Restoration of this organ to the norm of the Creator."

Then we reset all previous connections with all other cells and organs by means of the pituitary gland. We do this by giving the pituitary gland a command. We say:

"Restoration of all connections of this organ with all other organs."

Now we enter in the time and the date and send everything into infinity. We say (for example):

"4:30 p.m. on May 1st, 2010."

And then we send all positive information into infinity.

© Svetlana Smirnova, 2012

10. The Spine and its Points of Energy-Information

(Nadeshda Korolova, Vadim Korolov)

There are points of energy-information located along the length of the spine. Energy and information flow to these points (Fig. 6). Under normal conditions the energy informative points in the area of the neck are located 2 cm (approx. 13/16 in.) and those in other areas 2.5 cm (almost 1 in.) above the surface of the physical body. The most important points are:

- 3rd cervical vertebra
- 7th cervical vertebra
- 8th thoracic vertebra

What this means is that these are the points that are disrupted most often for an enormous stream of information flows to these points. They are the most sensitive points on the spine. Negative information from the external world can also have an effect upon these points. In relation to man, the external world is the macrocosm. Here, too, you can go out to macro level by saying:

"I go out to the macro level and direct an impulse to my physical body to transform all negative interconnections that it perceives."

© Svetlana Smirnova, 2012

Technology for Working with the Spine:

With problems of the spine, for example scoliosis, disc prolapse or vertebrae deterioration, we proceed as follows (Figures 7 & 8):

- Place spheres over the atlas and the area of the coccyx and set a program that each sphere expands the spine to the norm.

- Next place an archetype (ideal pattern) of the spine behind the actual spine that you are treating on the outer side of the back. This creates a space between the archetype and the spine itself.

- In front of the front side of the spine place the screen of the soul of the Creator.

- Picture a sphere containing living matter. Direct a stream of living matter into the space between the spine and the archetype to restore the spatial damage and a second stream through the spinal canal to restore all of the structures of the spine. Now set the program:

"Regeneration of the spine to the norm of the Creator."

© Svetlana Smirnova, 2012

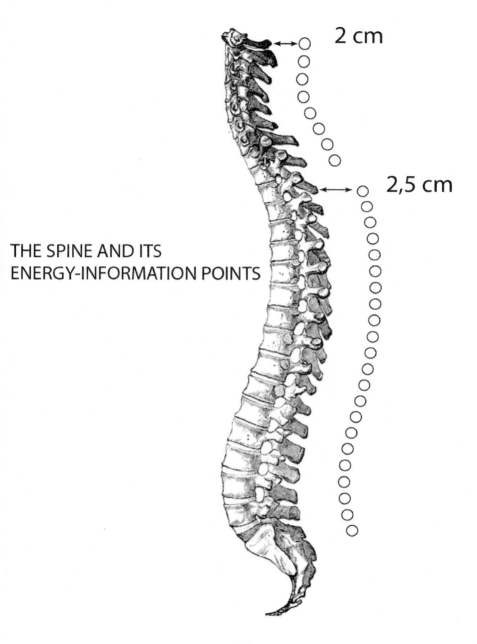

2 cm

2,5 cm

**THE SPINE AND ITS
ENERGY-INFORMATION POINTS**

Fig. 6

© Svetlana Smirnova, 2012

43

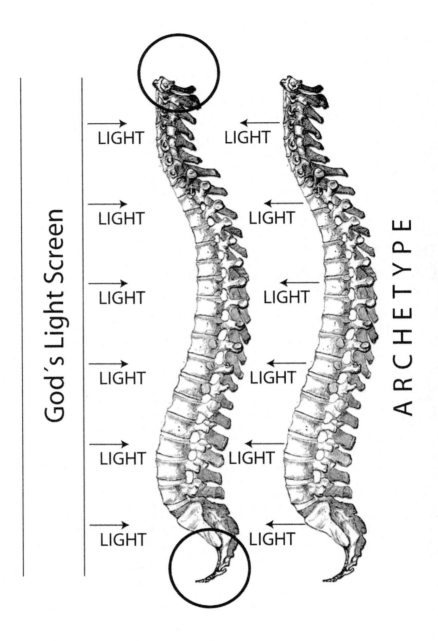

Fig. 7

© Svetlana Smirnova, 2012

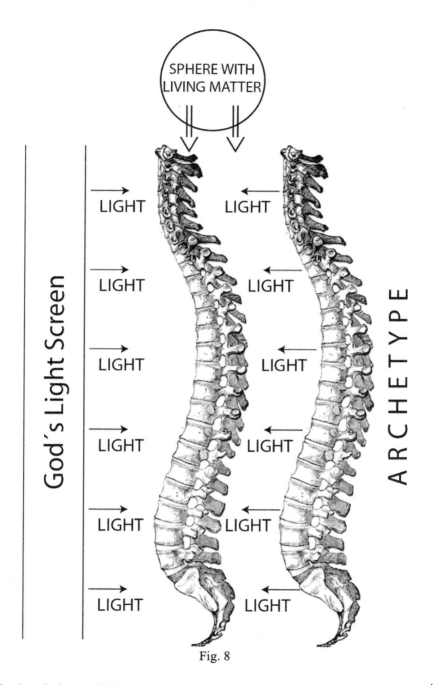

Fig. 8

© Svetlana Smirnova, 2012

- From the front of the thoracic region of the spine now extract an information cell from the bone structure and place it in the photon stream to effect the restoration of the cell structure of the spine. Set the program by saying:

"Restoration of the cell structure of the spine to the norm of the Creator."

- Enter in the time and the date and send everything into infinity.

We enter the time because this technology is based upon infinity. As soon as we enter the time into the cell, we are already imbuing space with a new and better quality. And because we have the knowledge that it is time that holds space together and can change it to the better, we can initiate a process of restoration to the norm.

© Svetlana Smirnova, 2012

The Technology with 4 Spheres

To adjust a vertebra so that it returns to its original position, we place 4 spheres, one on each side of the vertebra and connect the spheres with rays of light (Fig. 9). The light rays pull the opposing spheres together and move the herniated disc or dislocated vertebra back to its proper position. Through the spheres, which roll along the entire length of the spine, all of the vertebrae can be restored to their normed position and held there.

The spheres move at a very high speed. We set the corresponding program by saying:

"Restoration of the cell structure of the spine to the norm of the Creator."

Now we enter in the time and the date and send everything into infinity.

© Svetlana Smirnova, 2012

TECHNOLOGY WITH 4 SPHERES

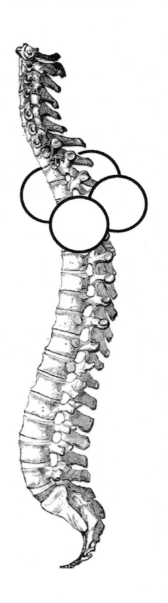

VIEW FROM ABOVE

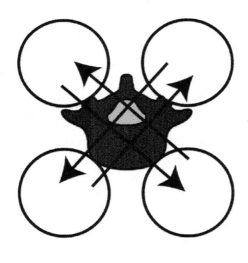

Fig. 9

© Svetlana Smirnova, 2012

11. Working with the Light Stream of the Creator

We use the light stream of the Creator for purification (of ourselves or others) from negative influences, information and emotions – after work or at the end of a stressful day or task. You can, for example, direct the stream over a building to harmonize the rooms and the people who are in them. You can place yourself or other people in the light stream of the Creator to clear the physical body of negativity and negative emotions.

Many people picture the light stream of the Creator vertically as a rainfall of golden color and others as a horizontal stream in which you can lie down. The important thing is to find your own, powerful image. We formulate our intention and set the program of guidance by saying:

"I place myself (or someone else) in the light stream of the Creator to cleanse and purify my (someone else's) physical body of all negative information and emotion."

Negative information and emotions do not conform to the divine norm. In order to harmonize rooms and the people who are in them, you can place the entire house or building, the office or any desired space in the light stream of the Creator. You can do the same with animals, plants or objects. We formulate our intention and set the program of guidance

© Svetlana Smirnova, 2012

by saying:

"I place the room in which I am right now (or: which I wish to harmonize for others and now visualize) in the light stream of the Creator in order to clear it and myself (us) of all negative information and emotions."

Finally, we enter in the date and the time and send everything into infinity.

© Svetlana Smirnova, 2012

12. The Extruder

(Nadeshda Korolova, Vadim Korolov)

The extruder (conveyer) was given us by the Creator for the removal of cancer cells, the removal of negative information and the removal of the informational structure of diseases. It norms and regenerates the cells of the organism and norms external events according to the Creator's plan.

The extruder consists of two screens that modulate the transition from the visible realm to that of the invisible. These screens are curved. If you were to complete their representation in the following diagram (Fig. 10), you would get two spheres: a lower sphere and an upper sphere, which also contains a sphere of living matter. Between the two spheres is the time cube.

The extruder works by taking hold of a negative cell of some organ and moving it in a clockwise spiral to the sphere with living matter. On the way to the living matter, the cell passes through both transition screens as it moves from the visible to the invisible world.

As it passes through the lower screen, the negative information on the disease in the cell is erased. In the region of the time cube, the information about the time is erased. As it passes through the upper screen, the information as to what organ this cell belongs to is erased.

In other words the cell reaches the sphere of living matter with damaged DNA. Here it is regenerated and restored according to the norm. Finally, it is returned, again in a clockwise spiral motion, to the organ from which it was taken.

As it passes back through the upper screen on the way back to the

© Svetlana Smirnova, 2012

51

body, the information as to which organ it belongs is restored to the cell. In the region of the time cube, the information about the time is restored and in passing through the lower screen, the information as to the state of health is given to the cell.

The cell is then returned to the organ from which it was taken.

When using this technology, we place the extruder over any particular organ or any particular situation. We formulate our intention and set the program for the guidance of events by saying:

"I set the extruder for the extraction of all negative information from my liver (or another organ or situation)."

Finally, we enter in the time and the date (or the calendar interval) and the information of the norm.

This method can transform any sort of information: a flu, a cold, inflammatory processes. We set the program for the guidance of events according to the pathogen and activate the extruder. We differentiate between an extruder for inner events such as diseases, personal disharmonies, etc. and a macro-extruder, which is much larger, for external events such as catastrophes, floods and hurricanes.

© Svetlana Smirnova, 2012

EXTRUDER

Sphere Containing Living Matter

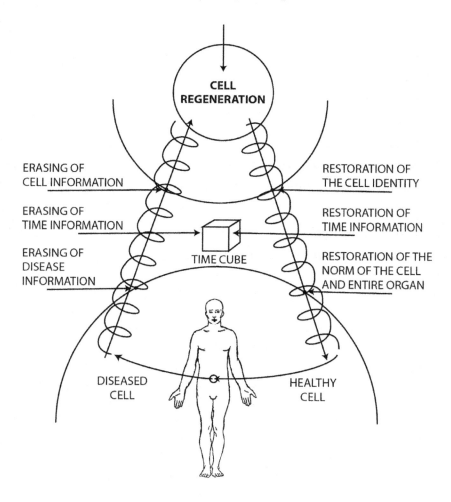

Fig. 10

© Svetlana Smirnova, 2012

53

13. The Cube–Cone–Cube System
(Grigori Grabovoi)

Our consciousness can make use of geometric forms very well. Bodies such as the cone, the sphere or the cube are especially suitable.

Working with Water:

Picture a cube in which a cone is located and inside the cone there is another smaller cube. This "Cube–Cone–Cube" system (Fig. 11) can be used to influence water (a liquid medium). We mentally purify the liquid from additives and harmful substances while structuring and purifying it to crystal clarity at the same time. In this manner we transform the information pertaining to the content and the structure of the water. This system can be used for the purification of any liquid.

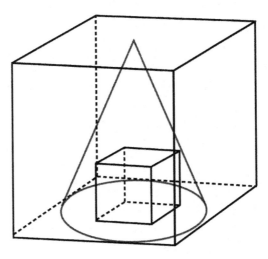

Fig. 11

© Svetlana Smirnova, 2012

Example for the purification of water:

Mentally place this geometric structure in the water flow. Say the following program for the guidance of events:

"I program this system for the purification of the water of poisons, toxins, microbes, and other additives with the goal of molecularly structuring this water according to how the Creator originally created water for eternity."

Say mentally or aloud:

"I place the Cube–Cone–Cube system in all waters, in rivers and lakes (or: in the epicenter of a catastrophe or areas with poisoned water) and initiate an immediate healing, the purification of poisons, toxins, radionuclides, or chemical substances. And with my love, together with the love of the Creator, I send the benefits of this technology into eternity and into infinity."

The Restoration of the Vitality of the Cell, the Blood and the Lymph:

It is possible in a similar manner to purify the blood, the hormonal system, the lymph fluids, or particular organs or cells, because our organism consists to approximately 80% of water and the information about a disease can be found in the water-based cellular fluids. You can also mentally construct new and healthy cells. You can make copies of these new structures and use them in yourself or others. When doing this, the old cells, including cancer cells, are repressed.

Mentally direct a living, normed cell from the Creator into the geometric structure of the Cube–Cone–Cube system. Then place the

© Svetlana Smirnova, 2012

entire complex into the aorta. Say the formula for a program for the guidance of events while picturing the blood in a blood red color:

"I program this system for the purification of the blood of poisons, toxins, microbes, other additives and contaminants with the goal of molecularly structuring it according to how it was originally made by the Creator."

Visualize how the normed cell from the Creator begins to multiply in order to restore the blood and to make you (or someone else) young again. Say mentally or aloud:

"I place the Cube–Cone–Cube system in the fluids of the entire living organism, in all inner organs, for an immediate healing, purification, regeneration and restoration to the form originally made by the Creator."

When working with the blood or lymph, add the following number sequence to the structure: 1843214.

Repeat this procedure a number of times and the normed cell of the Creator will repress all of the cells that do not correspond to the norm.

© Svetlana Smirnova, 2012

14. Concentrating on a Color
(Grigori Grabovoi)

Visualize the following colors:

     pink   yellow   green   red   blue   violet

Fix your gaze upon the color that stands out the most.

Now focus intensely and continuously for five minutes while holding the intention for a personal goal (the harmonizing of some circumstance). This concentration exercise recreates the sphere of important future events.

© Svetlana Smirnova, 2012

15. Ozone (O^3)
(Grigori Grabovoi)

For God the human being is His most important creation. Alone the shape of a human being already exhibits human properties. Grabovoi writes that if you take a puppet in a human shape and put it in a vacuum, then after a certain time oxygen is produced. This experiment was confirmed by American scientists. They could not explain this phenomenon.

It occurs, however, because the human body has the property of producing ozone (allotrope of oxygen). In the future when mankind has learned to consciously control this technology, he will have the ability to exist autonomously in any atmosphere.

The Technology of Working with Ozone:

Picture a pyramid located inside the 5-meter sphere (Fig 12). A small sphere sits on its apex. This is the sphere of the soul of man. The pyramid is the pyramid of the soul of the Creator – the light of the absolute, the light of the Creator.

The pyramid opens slightly and out of it come the light of the absolute and purifies the sphere of the soul. We see how the sphere is purified, how it begins to shine and is filled more and more with light.

After the sphere is filled with bright light, the pyramid opens further and the sphere sinks into the pyramid. This is the moment that ozone is produced. It is released in order to transform the negative cell information into something positive. The purifying quality of the ozone

58

© Svetlana Smirnova, 2012

itself restores the cells to the norm of the Creator.

We formulate our intention and set the program for the guidance of events by saying:

"I see diseased cells, a tumor.
I choose the necessary amount of ozone
and with the ozone take hold
of the diseased cells and the tumor."

The cells are literally devoured by the ozone. The entire tumor tissue begins to char and turn dark. Now we increase the concentration of the ozone in order to transform these cells into healthy tissue.

This technology works very effectively in oncology.

© Svetlana Smirnova, 2012

OZONE

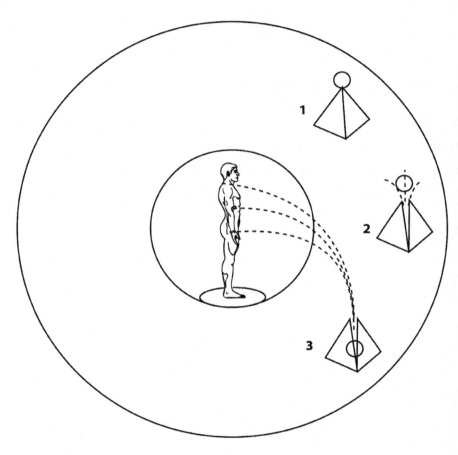

Fig. 12

© Svetlana Smirnova, 2012

16. Energetic Space Clearing
(Grigori Grabovoi)

Negative or stagnant energy always collects in the corners of a room. We use the following method to energetically clear a room or some space:

- Picture a small sphere in every corner of the room.

- Next visualize a large sphere in the center of the room.

- Mentally connect the small spheres in the corners with the large sphere in the center of the room.

- Finally, visualize that the negative energies of room flow from the small spheres into the large sphere and from there are carried upwards in a stream of energy to the realm of the Creator where they are transformed.

We say:

"I clear this room of all negative information."

© Svetlana Smirnova, 2012

17. The Restoration of Teeth
(Arcady Petrov)

The restoration of a single tooth or a number of teeth does not necessarily solve a person's problems. The primary question remains as to what degree the root cause of the disease has been dealt with. This question leads to a deeper understanding of the situation because the diseased tooth in many cases is only protecting one from an even greater destruction of the organism.

If a tooth is restored before the causes of the disease have been understood, then the problem can be transferred to a different organ where it can appear in a more serious form, particularly if the situation is not immediately recognized. It is important to know that restoration of teeth and hair are two of the most complicated regenerative processes. Of particular interest for this work are the stem cells, cells that in the process of replicating are capable of creating structures for every function and every organ.

Now all organs of the body have inner connections, including the teeth. Psychosomatic medicine has shown that particular teeth stand in relationship to particular organs. The disruption of the inner connections leads to a disruption of the external connections – and vice versa. If for example a person is aggressive, the liver could suffer from this and eventually the tooth that is connected with the liver starts to hurt.

The Technology for the Restoration of Teeth:
The goal of this work is the complete restoration of the teeth to the

© Svetlana Smirnova, 2012

norm through the method of regeneration. In this process we start with the stem cells.

Through our intention we construct a hologram of a healthy tooth. We do this by entering into one of its chromosomes with our consciousness. We illuminate the energy-information matrix of the hologram of the healthy tooth (Fig. 13).

CHROMOSOME

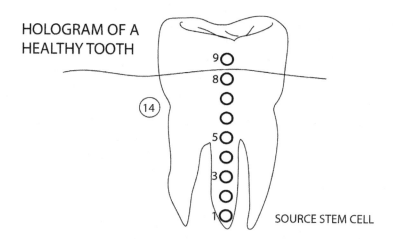

HOLOGRAM OF A HEALTHY TOOTH

SOURCE STEM CELL

© Svetlana Smirnova, 2012

We take a stem cell from the bone marrow and transplant it in the root of the tooth (Fig. 14).

Through our consciousness we give an impulse from the soul for the building up of a cell cluster. We create two cells from the original ("source") stem cell. Now there are 3 cells. Next we create two more. Now there are 5 cells. Next come an additional 3 cells and now we have 8 cells altogether (Fibonacci sequence). This cluster of cells creates a first "germ" or "nucleus" for the tooth.

Next we enter the code "differentiation," that is, we activate the transformation of the stem cells, which in the course of personal development have remained identical to their original state and are still non-specialized, into specialized cells for particular tissues and particular organs.

Next we give an impulse from the source stem cell for the creation of the ninth cell. After the creation of the ninth cell, the division of the "real" stem cells begins and they start to create the substances of the tooth (Fig. 15).

In order to accelerate the building up of the tooth substance, we picture additional "source" cells or cells with living matter. We activate them with an impulse from our consciousness.

With help of the thyroid gland, we restore the connection of the regenerated tooth to its related organs (according to the norm of the Creator) by saying:

"Restoration of the connection of this tooth to all related organs."

Silvery-white threads form from the thyroid to the restored tooth.

64 © Svetlana Smirnova, 2012

This technology can be applied to any other teeth for which regeneration is desired.

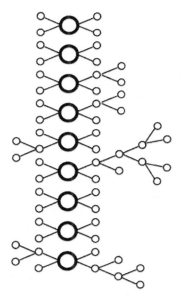

Fig. 15

© Svetlana Smirnova, 2012

18. Concentration on a Point

All matter in this world is made from concentrated light. You can see this light. It is everywhere – in everything – and can never be extinguished.

Method for working with a point:

Position the point (see below) about 2 meters (approx. 6½ feet) in front of you such that you can comfortably direct your focus upon it.

- Focus on the point until you notice that a dynamic halo begins to shine around its circumference.

- Continue to concentrate and make an effort to keep your focus on the point and its shining halo.

- You will notice that several bright spheres appear next to the point. These will start moving faster and faster around the shining middle point.

- The point of information has come to life and energy centers have developed around it, all of which take on psychic characteristics as well as the ability to create a new level of reality through the medium of the consciousness of the observer.

- At the moment this occurs, the black point will lift off of the

© Svetlana Smirnova, 2012

paper and in the background there will appear what seems to be an open and deep space. The point continues to float and can also change its position under the influence of one's thoughts.

In the next stage of this focus, it is better to concentrate upon a light-colored point (white, yellow, golden, silver, etc.).

Working with a light-colored point has its special qualities. While focusing, a blinking effect occurs. First the point appears and then it disappears again. Around the point there is again a bright, shining halo, that is, the area around the point becomes much brighter than the rest of the paper. It simply begins to shine.

This means that under your focus the light concentrates and condenses itself into a sphere. In contrast to being a wave, it switches into the state of a corpuscle (the smallest mass particle of bound light).

Through this phenomenon invisible objects (atoms, molecules, etc.) become visible. This is the mechanism of the appearance of the invisible world.

© Svetlana Smirnova, 2012

68

© Svetlana Smirnova, 2012

19. The Restoration of the Digestive System
(Grigori Grabovoi)

We start with the situation at the onset of the disease or, in other words, the original information of the disease. Let's say it has the form of a cylinder. The basis of the cylinder rests on a flat plane (Fig. 16) and has a diameter and height of 2 cm (approx. ¾ of an inch).

The information of the ideal form, the future event (e.g. the stomach-intestinal tract is restored, there is no cancer, there is no tumor/ulcer, etc.) is carried by a sphere, also with a diameter of 2 cm. This sphere is located directly opposed to the cylinder on the other side of the plane. So on the one side is the sphere with a diameter of 2 cm and on the other the cylinder with a diameter of 2 cm.

Now we extract all of the negative information out of the digestive system and put it into the cylinder. Next we remove the cylinder, which has become enlarged (radius of 2 cm), and put it into a silvery-white cube outside of the 5-meter sphere for the transformation of the negative information into positive information (Fig. 17). Then we place the sphere with the norm of the Creator into the digestive system (or the 3rd chakra). Next we send light into the entire process.

The sphere starts to spin in a clockwise direction.

© Svetlana Smirnova, 2012

WORKING WITH THE DIGESTIVE SYSTEM
5 METER SPHERE

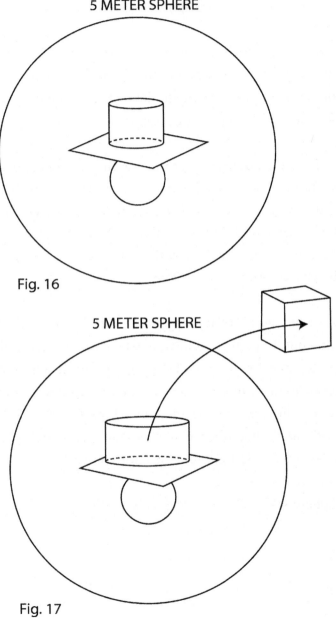

Fig. 16

5 METER SPHERE

Fig. 17

© Svetlana Smirnova, 2012

20. The Structure of the "Purification of the Soul"
(On a Lecture by Grigori Grabovoi – March 3rd, 2004)

"It is possible to reach a point where the soul is crystal clear. If such a person were to appear in the epicenter of a nuclear explosion, the entire informational base of the explosion would be so transformed that it would be as if no explosion took place. A crystal clear soul can do such a thing. For this reason all of the technologies that we create lead a person to that point where the soul becomes crystal clear. Those structures that are placed into the soul are transferred from the inner into the external world."

The technology for the creation of the immortal physical body was given to the world by Grigori Grabovoi in his lecture "On the Love of God."

As soon as the entire structure of the soul is transferred from the invisible to the visible world, a person becomes immediately immortal. The technologies that build up the physical body are technologies of deliverance. Within the body we have something, which is at the same time a cell of God. It is the only cell of the body that does not tolerate any change and carries within itself the functions of the divine origin. This cell is located under the left shoulder blade.

Try right now to sense the presence of this cell, to feel it, to see it. It is through this cell that divine love, the love that also builds up the entire physical body, flows into man. Picture yourself taking in this stream of love. Through this visualization you are in fact bringing this stream into

© Svetlana Smirnova, 2012

yourself through the "God cell." Feel how the stream of love and how divine love fills you through and through.

The point from which our love flows into the outer world is located below the chest. Everything, which is behind us, is our inner world, for our back is the representation of the soul.

In the inner, invisible world we first intensify love and then we release it into our surroundings. In other words, we give our love to all of the people around us and the world that surrounds us, because the world is giving this love to us the whole time.

After a certain time you will feel your love begins to flow from you to the entire surrounding world. When the space of love that exists within you is filled up, and it is continuously filled by the love of the Creator, your love begins to flow to others and you can feel how it flows out of you. Because of this joyous state, you can in this moment feel the love of others and the love of the world in return.

While you are intensifying the stream of love and drawing it into yourself, you can have a feeling of bliss in the God cell. This cell, which is located on our back, is – because it is eternal – unchangeable. While you are drawing the stream of love to yourself, try to connect the stream to the cells in the immediate vicinity. Fill the surrounding cells with the same love that you perceive in the God cell.

Svetlana Smirnova and Sergey Jelezky

© Svetlana Smirnova, 2012

The SVET-Center
for Spiritual Technologies

Goal and task of the Center: the spreading of the teachings of Grigori Grabovoi on the deliverance and eternal harmonious development of all people.

SVET provides information on the nature of the soul, the spirit and consciousness.

On the basis of the teaching on "general deliverance," technologies are provided for the reuniting of man with the Creator, technologies that lead one beyond all forms of structure.

Spiritual technologies are provided for the understanding of the building of the eternal physical body. Essentially every person can learn these technologies and acquire the ability to pass them on to others.

The Center offers educational courses and health therapy based upon this knowledge.

SVET teaches how to see the divine order underlying the events occurring around us and how to restore your health through your own efforts. For from our point of view, there are no incurable diseases.

© Svetlana Smirnova, 2012

Svetlana Smirnova

The neurologist and homeopath Svetlana Smirnova was born in Omsk (Sibiria). She graduated from the state medical college and then worked for ten years as a doctor in the neurological department of the state medical clinic in Omsk. Since 1995, she lives in Hamburg where she founded together with Sergey Jelezky the SVET-Zentrum (Center) for Spiritual Technologies. She teaches seminars and workshops in Hamburg and other places in Europe for interested people from all walks of life.

Sergey Jelezky

After graduating from the College of Technology in Omsk, Sergey Jelezky worked there and later in Hamburg as a professional artist and designer in his own atelier. Together with Svetlana Smirnova, he studied "Geovoyager" (the structuring of consciousness) at "Fond A. N. Petrov," a school for clairvoyance, then at "Hope," the Center for Spiritual Technologies, N.A. Koroleva and W.A. Korolev, and at The Center for Spiritual Technologies "Arigor," I.W. Arepjev (Moscow).

74

© Svetlana Smirnova, 2012

Notes

Jelezky Publishing

www.jelezky-publishing.com

First English Edition, January 2012

© 2012 English Language Edition

SVET Center, Hamburg

Svetlana Smirnova

www.svet-centre.eu

Edition: 2012- 1, 26.01.2012

ISBN: 978-3-943110-34-0

CPSIA information can be obtained at www.ICGtesting.com
Printed in the USA
BVOW06s1748190815

414010BV00008B/111/P